SO-BRM-700

Too Bright to See

&

Alma

Too Bright to See

& Alma

Poems by

LINDA GREGG

Graywolf Press

Copyright © 2002 by Linda Gregg

Publication of this volume is made possible in part by a grant provided by the Minnesota State Arts Board, through an appropriation by the Minnesota State Legislature, a grant from the Wells Fargo Foundation Minnesota, and by a grant from the National Endowment for the Arts. Significant support has also been provided by the Bush Foundation; Marshall Field's Project Imagine with support from Target Foundation; the McKnight Foundation; and other generous contributions from foundations, corporations, and individuals. To these organizations and individuals we offer our heartfelt thanks.

Support for this volume has been provided by the Jerome Foundation.

Too Bright to See was originally published by Graywolf Press in 1981.

Alma was originally published by Random House in 1985.

Published by Graywolf Press
250 Third Avenue North, Suite 600
Minneapolis, Minnesota 55401
All rights reserved.

www.graywolfpress.org

Published in the United States of America
Printed in Canada

ISBN 978-1-55597-357-5

2 4 6 8 9 7 5 3

Library of Congress Control Number: 2001088676

Cover design: Christa Schoenbrodt, Studio Haus

Cover photograph: Kore, Greek, Archaic period.
Acropolis Museum, Athens, Greece.
Nimatallah/Art Resource, NY

CONTENTS

Too Bright to See

PART THREE: AFTER THAT

Alma

Too Bright to See

FOR JACK GILBERT
IT WAS LIKE BEING ALIVE TWICE

TOO BRIGHT TO SEE

PART I

Alma

WE MANAGE MOST WHEN
WE MANAGE SMALL

What things are steadfast? Not the birds.
Not the bride and groom who hurry
in their brevity to reach one another.
The stars do not blow away as we do.
The heavenly things ignite and freeze.
But not as my hair falls before you.
Fragile and momentary, we continue.
Fearing madness in all things huge
and their requiring. Managing as thin light
on water. Managing only greetings
and farewells. We love a little, as the mice
huddle, as the goat leans against my hand.
As the lovers quickening, riding time.
Making safety in the moment. This touching
home goes far. This fishing in the air.

A GAME CALLED FEAR

The young cows run in the sound of the river,
making a noise on the grass
clumsy but full of gaiety. Not like the water.
There is the sound of birds in the white air.
The road is wet with rain,
the trees still and quiet.
The young cows are not afraid, I can tell you.
They stop and look together in one direction,
then run to the other end of the field
as if they were playing a game called fear.
The sky is silent and the river is loud
this time of year.

THE GIRL I CALL ALMA

The girl I call Alma who is so white
is good, isn't she? Even though she does not speak,
you can tell by her distress that she is
just like the beach and the sea, isn't she?
And she is disappearing, isn't that good?
And the white curtains, and the secret smile
are just her way with the lies, aren't they?
And that we are not alone, ever.
And that everything is backwards
otherwise.
And that inside the no is the yes. Isn't it?
Isn't it? And that she is the god who perishes:
the food we eat, the body we fuck,
the loose net we throw out that gathers her.
Fish! Fish! White sun! Tell me we are one
and that it's the others who scar me,
not you.

whose voice?

an act of distancing?

questions, questionable

THE CHORUS SPEAKS HER WORDS
AS SHE DANCES

You are perishing like the old men. Already your arms are gone,
your legs filled with scented straw tied off at the knees.
Your hair hacked off. How I wish I could take on each part
of you as it leaves. Sweet mouse princess, I would sing
like a nightingale, higher and higher to a screech
which the heart recognizes, which the helpless stars enjoy—
like the sound of the edge of grass.

I adore you. I take you seriously, even if I am alone in this.
If you had arms, you would lift them up I know. Ah, Love,
what knows that?

(How tired and barren I am.)
Mouse eyes. Lady with white on her face. What will the world do
without you? What will the sea do?
How will they remember the almond flowers? And the old man,
smiling, holding up the new lamb: whom will he hold it up to?
What will the rough men do after their rounds of drinks
and each one has told his story? How will they get home
without the sound of the shore anymore?

(I think my doll is the sole survivor, my Buddha mouse, moon
princess, amputee who still has the same eyes.
With her song that the deer sings when it is terrified.
That the rabbits sing, grass sings, fish, the sea sings:
a sound like frost, like sleet, high keening, shrill squeak.
Zo-on-na, Kannon, I hold each side of her deeply affected face
and turn on the floor.

This song comes from the bottom of the hill at night, in summer.
From a distance as fine as that first light on those islands.
As the lights on the dark island which held still while our ship
came away. This is the love song that lasts through history.
I am a joke and a secret here, and I will leave.
It is morning now. The light whitens her face more than ever.)

GNOSTICS ON TRIAL

Let us make the test. Say God wants you
to be unhappy. That there is no good.
That there are horrors in store for us
if we do manage to move toward Him.
Say you keep Art in its place, not too high.
And that everything, even eternity, is measurable.
Look at the photographs of the dead,
both natural (one by one) and unnatural
in masses. All tangled. You know about that.
And can put Beauty in its place. Not too high,
and passing. Make love our search for unhappiness,
which is His plan to help us.
Disregard that afternoon breeze from the Aegean
on a body almost asleep in the shuttered room.
Ignore melons, and talking with friends.
Try to keep from rejoicing. Try
to keep from happiness. Just try.

THERE SHE IS

When I go into the garden, there she is.
The specter holds up her arms to show
that her hands are eaten off.
She is silent because of the agony.
There is blood on her face.
I can see she has done this to herself.
So she would not feel the other pain.
And it is true, she does not feel it.
She does not even see me.
It is not she anymore, but the pain itself
that moves her. I look and think
how to forget. How can I live while she
stands there? And if I take her life
what will that make of me? I cannot
touch her, make her conscious.
It would hurt her too much.
I hear the sound all through the air
that was her eating, but it is on its own now,
completely separate from her. I think
I am supposed to look. I am not supposed
to turn away. I am supposed to see each detail
and all expression gone. My God, I think,
if paradise is to be here
it will have to include her.

*women
disembodied,
dehumanized*

THE WOMAN WHO LOOKS FOR
HER LOST SISTER SHE SAYS

She walks all the time in the Heart Ward.
She makes no sound. She is always alone.
If she is looking in the toilet stall and you come in
she leaves. She calls you Dear.
I was thinking of giving her my flowers.
Just now she came over and said,
"You don't have to be writing all the time, Dear."
I said, "Do you have any flowers?"
She said, "No Dear."
I said, "Do you want any flowers?"
She said, "No, no flowers Dear."
I said, "Don't you want any flowers at all?"
"No," she said, "it's too late for flowers Dear."

AT THE SHORE

Naked women are being dragged
down the sandstone shelving
on their backs, very slowly.
With ropes tied to each foot separately
so the legs close and spread open
as they are moved.
When they cry out or shout down
at the men sitting in the lifeguard chairs
looking at them through the gun sights,
the sounds, no matter how angry or foul,
curve and billow like a wave: coming
to the men on a soft wind
caressingly, like sirens singing.

*subverting the
siren myth ...
What men think is
pleasure actually = pain*

THE BECKETT KIT

I finally found a way of using the tree.
If the man is lying down with the sheep
while the dog stands, then the wooden tree
can also stand, in the back, next to the dog.

They show their widest parts
(the dog sideways, the tree frontal)
so that being next to each other
they function as a landscape.

I tried for nearly two months to use the tree.
I tried by putting the man,
standing of course, very far from the sheep
but in more or less the same plane.
At one point I had him almost off the table
and still couldn't get the tree to work.
It was only just now I thought of a way.

I dropped the wooden sheep from a few inches
above the table so they wouldn't bounce.
Some are on their backs but they serve
the same as the ones standing.
What I can't get over is their coming right
inadvertently when I'd be content with any solution.

Ah, world, I love you with all my heart.
Outside the open window, down near the Hudson,
I can hear a policeman talking to another
through the car radio. It's eleven stories down
so it must be pretty loud.
The sheep, the tree, the dog, and the man
are perfectly at peace. And my peace is at peace.
Time and the earth lie down wonderfully together.

The blacks probably do rape the whites in jail   *woah...*
as Bill said in the coffee shop watching the game
between Oakland and Cincinnati. And no doubt
Karl was right that we should have volunteered
as victims under the bombing of Hanoi.

A guy said to Mishkin, "If you've seen all that,
how can you go on saying you're happy?"

SIGISMUNDO

The fete confused me. Guests played the part of gods.
There was a woman with white skin who stood
with her pale robe open all night throwing roses.
A lady found me in the only quiet room and demanded
I take her to him. I refused even when she begged,
and went down by the water to think of something else.
Sun rose that morning on the torches.
Cool air over the tepid sea. Sigismundo the Beautiful.
Out for himself. Torturer of doves. A killer of cities.
Killer of wife before breakfast. Sigismundo,
who built a church to a woman not beautiful,
with roses cut in the stone.
All through my boyhood I was told I'd walk hand in hand
with death. I chose the good, and cried
when they marred the statues.
But there is nothing, nothing to say about my life.
Unmerciful Sigismundo did many wrongs and his people loved him
and he will live forever. I who go down like Persephone
with my accomplishments of silence and weeping unrecorded,
even I if I were a girl would answer Yes, I know how to swim.
Lie for the chance to drown in that blue water of his.
Sigismundo.

THE POET GOES ABOUT HER BUSINESS

for Michele (1966–1972)

Michele has become another dead little girl. An easy poem.
Instant Praxitelean. Instant seventy-five-year-old photograph
of my grandmother when she was a young woman with shadows
I imagine were blue around her eyes. The beauty of it.
Such guarded sweetness. What a greed of bruised gardenias.
Oh Christ, whose name rips silk, I have seen raw cypresses
so dark the mind comes to them without color.
Dark on the Greek hillside. Dark, volcanic, dry and stone.
Where the oldest women of the world are standing dressed in black
up in the branches of fig trees in the gorge
knocking with as much quickness as their weakness will allow.
Weakness which my heart must not confuse with tenderness.
And on the other side of the island a woman
walks up the path with a burden of leaves on her head,
guiding the goats with sounds she makes up,
and then makes up again. The other darkness is easy:
the men in the dreams who come in together to me with knives.
There are so many traps, and many look courageous.
The body goes into such raptures of obedience.
But the huge stones on the desert resemble
nobody's mother. I remember the snake.
After its skin had been cut away and it was dropped,
it started to move across the clearing.
Making its beautiful waving motion.
It was all meat and bone. Pretty soon it was covered with dust.
It seemed to know exactly where it wanted to go.
Toward any dark trees.

GOETHE'S DEATH MASK

The face is quite smooth
everywhere except the eyes,
which are bulges
like ant hills someone tried to draw
eyes on. It is normal, of course,
that the mouth is shut
like a perfect sentence.
But there is nothing of Italy
or the rooms. As though it were
all a lie. As if he had not fed there
at all. I suppose there was never a choice.
If the happiness lasts,
it is the smoothness. The part
we do not notice. The language he made
was from the bruises. What lasted
are the eyes. Something ugly
and eaten into. What a mess his eyes are.

*happiness goes
unnoticed/
unrecollected*

ALMA IN ALL SEASONS

She has arms instead of breasts.
And there are no stars.
I put her in this box
because it is summer.
And put a cloth with flowers
sewn on it over her. Rabbit fur
under and around her sides.
To make summer for her.
She is not warm automatically.
The stationery box is light blue.
The jar with water holding roses
is turquoise. I see her looking out.
Her eyes are dark. Hot air sucks
my curtain out the window
and lets it drop.
Her eyes look on nothing.
She must be thinking. She must be
feeling. She does not remember people.
It is summer but the same was true
when there was snow.

DIFFERENT NOT LESS

All of it changes at evening
equal to the darkening,
so that night-things may have their time.
Each gives over where its nature is essential.
The river loses all but a sound.
The bull keeps only its bulk.
Some things lose everything.
Colors are lost. And trees mostly.
At a time like this we do not doubt our dreams.
We believe the dead are standing along the other edge
of the river, but do not go to meet them.
Being no more powerful than they were before.
We see this change is for the good,
that there is completion, a coming around.
And we are glad for the amnesty.
Modestly we pass our dead in the dark,
and history—the Propylaea to the right
and above our heads. The sun, bull-black
and ready to return, holds back so the moon,
delicate and sweet, may finish her progress.
We look into the night, or death, our loss,
what is not given. We see another world alive
and our wholeness finishing.

PART II

The Marriage
and After

THE WIFE

My husband sucks her tits.
He walks into the night, her Roma, his being alive.
Toward that other love. I wait in the hotel
until four. I lurch from the bed
talking to myself, watch my face in the mirror.
I change my eyes, making them darker.
Take it easy, I say. It is a long time to wait in,
this order of reality. My presence stings.
I grow specific without consequence.

THE ISLAND OF KOS

Nothing but wilderness around.
Two days of spring and then days of cold.
The sea flooding the road.
Wild heaving against poetry.
Breaking boats on the rocks.
Spill, spill and pour against the mountain.
Flooding the winter wheat.

Wait for me! Wait for me! You are far ahead.
I think the wilderness has won. We are silent
in the house while the wind rises and wanes.
I came here not knowing there was something
that could be lost. That could be taken.

In order to get to sleep, I think:
Go to sleep little goat. Your first week is over.
Go to sleep now.

TROUBLE IN THE PORTABLE MARRIAGE

"What whiteness will you add to this whiteness, what candor?"

We walk the dirt road toward town through the clear evening.
The sky is apricot behind the black cane. Pink above,
and dull raspberry on the Turkish hills across the water.
The Aegean is light by the shore, then dark farther out.
I cannot distinguish now which is light and which is color.
I go up the road on my bicycle, floating in the air:
the moon enlarging and decreasing, moving all the time
close to my head. I stop at the bridge.
Get off and sit on the rail because I remember
I have no money. After a while you come.
Your hand touches me and then withdraws.
We talk about why the moon changes size, and I think
how I'd smelled it. Like sweet leaf smoke,
like sweet wood burning. We go toward town together,
me riding and you walking. Feeling the silk and paleness
of the air. No one passes us the whole length of the road.

THE SMALL LIZARD

My lizard just beyond the lamp's shine
is a gentle lizard.
Is the color of an old peach.
Has lived with me all summer
and kept his tail.

(I am a little better, but love is leaving.
I who never loved birds am growing wings.)

When I move, my lizard does not.
But watches and makes himself ready.
The moon has gone above my window now,
and will go over the rooftop.

(Now, when I could help, I hold back.
My heart is sad, not wanting to fly.
Who moves from grace by choice?)

We are three stages. The lizard,
more than I or the moon, is the soul
developed. The moon will dim
and I will change;
but this immortal lizard will stay
breathing in this stone room,
without evidence.

TOGETHER IN GREECE

I was sitting on the steps of the cinema
when he introduced his pretty friend.
The few bare bulbs showed how dark and barren it was.
I got up and left the town.
Went out with no attitude prepared.
I went to a winnowing ring in the fields and lay down,
where all day they ran horses and donkeys
over the barley, a farmer running with his hands tied
to them. Knew the air was cold and saw myself there.
Realized I was strange.
When the moon wanted me to sing
with my mouth open, I refused.
I knew Jack was looking for me. Stayed silent.
Heard him calling my name in the village streets.
Finally came out of the fields
and walked toward him. Dark and huge.
My head ached from the sounds I did not make.
It was more frightening than living.
I went to him, with that singing in me.

infidelity?
misunderstanding?

CLASSICISM

The nights are very clear in Greece.
When the moon is round we see it completely
and have no feeling.

ALMA WATCHING HER HUSBAND

Halfway through the scene I could not decide
whether Alma should react or go on standing there
by the window of her dark room, her back to us
and the bright summer night above the roofs beyond.
She was looking into the apartment across the courtyard
as they finished making love and the woman
climbed down the ladder from the high bed,
shining in the candlelight. Maybe Alma
should lie on the floor with her face showing.
Or smash the tulips, kneel crying alongside,
then quickly sweep them up. But I wanted something
more tenuous. I went outside. The air smelled
like cardamom. Students were singing in the street.
It was already morning. I wrote it all down:
the kind of daylight at midnight in Denmark
and the kind at four in the morning. Maybe Alma
would sit with her legs out the window watching
the birds overhead. When I got back, the man downstairs
was crying because his wife had just died of cancer.
He used to grab Alma when she came home from ballet class
and weep in her hair. Maybe I could show Alma's husband
for the ending. Walking across the city,
over the bridges and along the moats to his workroom.
He would make soup and put it on the cast-iron stove.
Pour tea and begin to work. A boy might come by
from the next cabin and say they had moved the trumpet
player into a soundproof room facing out on the marsh.
Then I knew she would just go on standing there.

(handwritten note left margin: alma becomes I?)

(handwritten note bottom: inaction = giving in?)

WHOLE AND WITHOUT
BLESSING

What is beautiful alters, has undertow.
Otherwise I have no tactics to begin with.
Femininity is a sickness. I open my eyes
out of this fever and see the meaning
of my life clearly. A thing like a hill.
I proclaim myself whole and without blessing,
or need to be blessed. A fish of my own
spirit. I belong to no one. I do not move.
Am not required to move. I lie naked on a sheet
and the indifferent sun warms me.
I was bred for slaughter, like the other
animals. To suffer exactly at the center,
where there are no clues except pleasure.

GROWING UP

I am reading Li Po. The tv is on
with the sound off.
I've seen this movie before.
I turn on the sound just for a moment
when the man says, "I love you."
Then turn it off and go on reading.

SUMMER IN A SMALL TOWN

When the men leave me,
they leave me in a beautiful place.
It is always late summer.
When I think of them now,
I think of the place.
And being happy alone afterwards.
This time it's Clinton, New York.
I swim in the public pool
at six when the other people
have gone home.
The sky is grey, the air hot.
I walk back across the mown lawn
loving the smell and the houses
so completely it leaves my heart empty.

UNACCOUNTABLE

—They meant her to last forever.
—She invariably did kill someone every
voyage she made.
—She was unaccountable.

(Conrad, *The Brute*)

Many things are made of pride.
She will be alone in her bath washing off
some man's sweat before you come home.
You know what power the brute has now.
There is nothing to do against it.
The husband comes home
and if he is in a good mood
goes to her,
thinking of excitement.
She lifts her arms with a cunning smile
and he licks the sweat off her sides
and belly.
She pinches off a short dark hair
stuck by her navel and they laugh.
The laugh dies.
And the next joke dies
until neither can laugh fast enough,
for silence invades the empty heart
and the ripe roses are somewhere displaced
in the memory,
and the instincts run backwards.
The woman stares.
In the empty room she suddenly turns,
prepared to hear.
The husband looks down at his feet
as if trying to remember.

AFTER THAT

When the sun goes down and the world starts
to darken the three white geese do not.
Until the night really comes and covers them,
they are still white. Only perhaps waxier.

NO MORE MARRIAGES

Well, there ain't going to be no more marriages.
And no goddam honeymoons. Not if I can help it.
Not that I don't like men,
being in bed with them and all. It's the rest.
And that's what happens, isn't it? All those people
that get littler together. I want things
to happen to me the proper size.
The moon and the salmon and me and the fir trees,
they're all the same size and they live together.
I'm the worse part, but mean no harm.
I might scare a deer, but I can walk and breathe
as quiet as a person can learn.
If I'm not like my grandmother's garden
that smelled sweet all over and was warm
as a river, I do go up the mountain
to see the birds close and look
at the moon just come visible, and lie down
to look at it with my face open.
Guilty or not, though, there won't be no post-
cards made up of my life with Delphi on them.
Not even if I have to eat alone all these years.
They're never going to do that to me.

*the moon &
Greece &
Stupid men*

EURYDICE

I linger, knowing you are eager (having seen
the strange world where I live)
to return to your friends
wearing the bells and singing the songs
which are my mourning.
With the water in them, with their strange rhythms.
I know you will not take me back.
Will take me almost to the world,
but not out to house, color, leaves.
Not to the sacred world that is so easy
for you, my love.

Inside my mind and in my body is a darkness
which I am equal to, but my heart is not.
Yesterday you read the Troubadour poets
in the bathroom doorway
while I painted my eyes for the journey.
While I took tiredness away from my face,
you read of that singer in a garden
with the woman he swore to love forever.

You were always curious what love is like.
Wanted to meet me, not bring me home.
Now you whistle, putting together
the new words, learning the songs
to tell the others how far you traveled for me.
Singing of my desire to live.

Oh, if you knew what you do not know
I could be in the world remembering this.
I did not cry as much in the darkness
as I will when we part in the dimness
near the opening which is the way in for you
and was the way out for me, my love.

NOW DESTROYED

I

The girl you speak of is lost,
managing to hold on only to objects,
with a wildness like pleading.
Small things.
Those she can carry with her
and care for. She does not want a plant.
It might die. She prefers photographs
of the Kore with dark eyes.
The Rheims Christ ("now destroyed").
A painting of an island when the sun,
going away, left the earth and Aegean
feminine for an hour.
What living is to her is painful.
Knowing life a dependency on things
which can be taken away, or forgotten.
She could be found dead in her urine
and they might throw everything out.

II

There is nothing like that here.
Just the rain, the road, the dim
morning light, and the birds singing
faster and faster.
I follow the river with my mind,
trying to learn feeling. When I lived
at Monolithos a man rode a burro
every morning and evening
to a church that was never used,
to keep the lamps lit.
He will continue doing that
even though I came back to America.

THE DEFEATED

I sat at the desk for a while fooling with my hair
and looking at the black birds on the bakery roof.
Pulled the curtain, put my hair back, and said
it's time to start. Now it's after three.
You are still on the bus, I guess, looking out
the window. Sleeping. Knowing your defeat
and eating lunch part by part so it will last
the whole journey.

I heard there are women who light candles
and put them in the sand. Wade out in dresses
carrying flowers. Here we have no hope.
The pregnant woman has the abortion and then
refuses to speak. Horses stall in their strength,
whitening patches of air with their breath.
There will be this going on without them.
Dogs bark or five birds fly straight up
to a branch out of reach.

I had warm pumpernickel bread, cheese and chicken.
It is sunny outside. I miss you. My head is tired.
John was nice this morning. Already what I remember
most is the happiness of seeing you. Having tea.
Falling asleep. Waking up with you there awake
in the kitchen. It was like being alive twice.
I'll try to tell you better when I am stronger.

What does the moth think when the skin begins to split?
Is the air an astonishing pain? I keep seeing the arms
bent. The legs smashed up against the breasts,
with her sex showing. The weak hands clenched.
I see the sad, unused face. Then she starts to stand up
in the opening out. I know ground and trees.
I know air. But then everything else stops
because I don't know what happens after that.

Just before dark the light gets dark. Violet
where my hands pull weeds around the Solomon's seals.
I see with difficulty what before was easy.
Perceive what I saw before
but with more tight effort. I am moon
to what I am doing and what I was.
It is a real beauty that I lived
and dreamed would be, now know
but never then. Can tell by looking hard,
feeling which is weed and what is form.
My hands are intermediary. Neither lover
nor liar. Sweet being, if you are anywhere that hears,
come quickly. I weep, face set, no tears, mouth open.

THE APPARENT

When I say transparency, I don't mean seeing through.
I mean the way a symbol is made when an X is drawn over O.
As the world moves when it is named. In the sense
of truth by consciousness, which we translate as *opposites.*
The space we breathe is also called distance.
Presence gives. Absence allows and calls,
until Presence holds the invisible, weeping.
Transparent in the way the heart sees old leaves.
As we become more like the hills by feeling.
I mean permanence. As when the deer and I
regard each other. Ah, there was no fear then.
When she went with her young from the meadow
back into the nearly night of the woods,
it was because the rain came down suddenly harder.

PART III

After That

NOT SINGING

When you stop looking at the garden,
the eye begins furtively to acknowledge the barren poplars
and the giant spruce and the firs.
And so it is with this maid in me not asking to be saved.
Another one takes her place. Neither merciful nor unmerciful.
There are almost no flowers to be looked at anyhow.
No flowers to bear having an opinion about.
And the more it rains the less flowers there are.
The flowers, they say, all along were the journey.
Like the branches thrown down before the little donkey feet
of Christ on the way to glory.
I would not have it different.
Ruin is everywhere. The plague of soft rain endless.
We sing of loss because the only voice they gave us
was song and reasoning. It is not love we are after.
No love. Not singing. But a somber thing.
A going to the opening and entering.

BLAKE

The sun is on the roof,
the laundry is drying in the light.
Air moves around me and I prepare.
Make a gift of myself. Make my feet soft,
and think of Blake riding
near the tops of the trees
past our house.

The bread is in the oven and we die.
The day is spread and we delay.
Blake already is in the sky.
What is joy in this dark room?
What is light to this?
All night the ghosts of disperse,
of chaos, flee through my dreaming.

I would not repent. Though the world
separated into all its parts
and could not go back.
Get out! Get out! Get out! I shouted,
until I could not tell if anything was left
to talk to that had ears. Still refused.
Then the sun smiled, and Christ smiled,
and my laundry grew soft in the warm wind.
There. See there. The world is good to me.
I am finished with knife and window.
My bed will be underground soon enough.
I will persist in this permanence
that flesh holds. The body smooth,
the voices speaking within.

TOO BRIGHT TO SEE

Blake comes down, calling me.
Says this is the time.
The sea is hitting the rocks.
The light is crushed and flies up,
back to the sun.
Rejoice in the breaking of the light.
Rejoice when you are two and one.
In the leaving and the coming home.
Rejoice in the room that awaits you,
empty except for the empty glass.

I fly up. Disappear inside of him.
It is grand. I see the simple cow,
a red-tailed hawk and a lamb.
The creek with the small fish in it,
and sounds of the sea at the edge of a field.
The sound of it lightly under the trees.
Birds whistling. Wind and leaves mixing
in the slightly swollen heat.
The sound of the sea in his mind.

The glass is spilling.
They both shine in that room,
water and spilling light.

THE GODS MUST NOT KNOW US

The signifying clouds at dawn
fill me. Open my spirit.
The shining of sun and moon
morning after morning
makes my heart serene.

(from *Shang-shu ta chuan* by Fu Sheng)

All the different kinds of light
give off light.
The light of the heart (sun).
The light of the mind (moon).
Longing and having make it all
possible for us.

But what the world gives disturbs,
this confusion of excess the world gives.
Morning comes again and again,
holding everything lovingly.
We cannot hold it all at once
this giving.

kalos is written over the heads of the gods
on the Greek vases. They like beauty so much
they fill the world with it.
Until the plenty makes our joy hesitate
and I fear they will know we do not have a place
big enough to handle so much.

TOO BRIGHT TO SEE

The world gives forth beauty
like the great, glad women in the dream.
It overwhelms us. Spills over.
I am afraid the earth will take it back
and part of myself will get lost
and I will not be a fitting gift.

The gods must not know us well or they would
not dance so openly, so happily before us.

excess of beauty → gluttony, sadness

THE GRUB

The almost transparent white grub moves
slowly along the edge of the frying pan.
The grease makes the only sound, loud
in the empty room. Even the rim is cooking him.
The worm stops. Raises his head slightly.
Lowers it, moving tentatively down the side.
He seems to be moving on his own time,
but he is falling by definition. He moves forward
touching the frying grease with his whole face.

THIS PLACE

There is a place in the desert which I keep making,
making the light blister and the shadows glow
with a red darkness. Making black a substance
invisible behind the red. Shadows
like those in a place built to be a stronghold
for pity's sake make me wonder why I put it there,
making sure of the heat and the blond lions
quivering against the blond sandstone so that
you almost cannot see them, or believe them
a mirage. Making water of them and moving them
closer to the rock. It makes me wonder why
I saw lions as guardians, angels flexing their jaws,
tightening against the walls for pity's sake.
And I cry out to them with my burned mouth
full of joy and wonder: "Pity, I have found you.
Pity, I bring you a present of my mind, complete
with the sweet smell of the King's garden
when you come into it from a small distance.
I have not made you up. You are here."
And the lions turn in the canyon I have made
with my voice, see me calling, and we move closer.

WHAT IF THE WORLD STAYS
ALWAYS FAR OFF

What if the world is taken from me?
If there is no recognition? My words unheard?
Keats wanted to write great poetry
and I am in the orchard all day.

The work is too hard and no one here
will do it. So they bring Jamaicans.
The men sometimes sing on their ladders.
Named Henry and George. "Yes, Boss," they say.
The bus brought them late this morning.
They not wanting to work because of the cold.
They walk slowly through the wet grass.
"Today we are not happy," they say going by me.

The grass is wet one to three hours.
Then dry. Sometimes everything is warm
and I wish the man I know would come
in his car and make love to me.

We do not speak much. Because of the work.
And because I am the only woman.
They see no women. Two months here picking apples.
Six in Florida cutting cane.

At night my body is so tired I don't want
to make love. I want to be alone and to sleep.
It is very beautiful in the fields under

She talks of the laborers w/
such anonymity and yet SHE'S
invisible ??

TOO BRIGHT TO SEE

the apple trees all day. I saw two night hawks
white with black wave designs counter to the wings.
The boss saw two hundred of them fly over
this valley once. Going south.
What if I continue unnoticed.

Foxes red and grey. Woodchucks. A pretty rabbit
on the road in the rain, confused and afraid.
Running suddenly toward the lights.

An apple has all colors. Even blue.
Much purple and maroon. (If there would be
no recognition and the world remains far away?)
The leaves are a duller green than the grass.
I pick macintosh, but there are forty kinds
on the land around. Three hundred acres
near the next town. This is autumn in Massachusetts.
Not my home. I heard of beauty in New England
and the people. Came looking for love.

Nobody talks to the Jamaicans. They are driven
to Safeway in the bus and brought back.
I saw one alone just standing by the woods.
"I send money to my mother if I feel like it,"
he said to impress me. About eighteen.
He will cut cane for the first time this year.
"I hear the bosses are mean," I said.
"We make more money," he said. "It is a longer time."

Are you lost if there is no recognition?
Is beauty home? Is fear or pain?
An old man who drives the truck and has a farm
of his own down the road said,
"I just help during the harvest.
I have everything except apples. Lots of squash."
It made me happy to know they still say harvest.

I am here with them for the harvest. Thirty-six.
A woman. Canning when there's time. It will be
very cold soon. Already there are dark rains.

touristy, yo. in the D.F.W. sense.

TOO BRIGHT TO SEE

STAYING ON

The geese go over
with a broken sound,
moving clumsily toward
their Troy. As she,
crouched down,
goes on picking
up the apples
under the trees.
Not proceeding anywhere.
Close to the ground
with bobcats, rabbits,
mice, woodchucks,
a doe with her young.
Arriving their way
into winter.

LILITH

I

The light is on my body also.
Even now when I am alone in the woods.
That is something they never tell you.
And I have always been alone.
Even when men found me and used me,
it never lasted. I knew lust
can be satisfied and I would be
returned to myself before long.
Would see everything as it was.
Dark trees, bright lights.
Speech only was lost.

II

I line up five stones on the ground.
I count them. I laugh
even though I am alone.
Remembering how the men never knew
how reasonable I am. Every day
I walk to the edge of the world
and look at the ocean.
And then return to my home.
It goes on like this.
They are afraid of the pain
they have given me. I made a dam
in the creek today and then took
the stones away. I make a fire
to keep warm when it is necessary.
How can they think I am crazy?

III

A woman comes to my door and asks for bread.
It is winter. I look at her face
and recognize myself. I say: Lady, you hurt me
with your pain. She sings: Are you afraid
when the branches scrape the windowpanes?
Are you? Never has there been more agreement
between anyone. Go away, I say. Go away.
And slam the door. I fall down crying
for anything but woman to ease my suffering.
Death would be more kind. I open the door.
She is standing there with tears on her face,
just like before. Unsure whether to start again.

IV

Statuary used to fill the gardens of rich
and powerful men. At the end in Paris
they were of women. That is all gone now.
The wars came. Lists of dead were horrible.
I walk through the fields of rotting bodies
at evening to get a bucket of water
to carry back to the house on my head.
Gradually there will be gardens again.
First for food and then also for flowers.

ornamental, useless?

AS WHEN THE
BLOWFISH PERISHING

As when the blowfish, perishing,
makes itself the greatest size,
the empty agoras and broken colosseums
repeat the supposition of a god
who worshipped a god. Pretending
those men were proportionate
to what they made. And they are. I think
of how you dream and dream and care
for the blood carried in silver bowls
out of the room. Of my diminishing
as the world makes love to me.
It is a long way from the rock to here.
There is a huge pile of dead people
and they will not sing. I wish so
you would come back.
We kept the courtesy an internal form
to have the beauty after.

SUN MOON KELP FLOWER OR GOAT

Later I would say, I have cut myself free from order,
statistics, and what not, what have you.
But I was never connected. To anything.
Marriage taught me to let go more. As if I knew
what I wanted. As if I were after something.
The *finally* was that year as I walked the island
every day. I could feel something extraordinary.
It was the same in me as outside me. I could say us:
The flat land I walked. The mountain approaching.
The blanching of everything living and dying.
Ruined hills and towns without roofs on the houses.
Men and women in black clothing offering water,
singing, being silent, laughing. Dying, as if that
were anything to us who were nature and beyond
suffering. What survives. The part which remains.
What is birth and death to sun, fish, kelp, eggs?
But there is kindness which feeds us another way,
with windlessness, empty heat, or the taste of grapes.

SKYLORD

for Harold Gregg (1906–1980)

The small hawk flutters fiercely upright,
shivering with great energy to stand so
in air over hills and their declivities.
Hunting mole, mouse and whom. Ally of wind,
owner of sky, elegant lord embracing what is
known and not known. A magnificence over us
which plunges for small life to eat. Dear gods,
you are dependent on the mouse that lives
with the hill's heartbeat and knows more,
much more by far, than your invisible school
of latitude and longitude. You must study
by compression of patience movement between
eyelids blinking. Must learn racing between
two heartbeats. And it takes you a long while
and humility and failure. Each time you come
close we look in awe of you. That the sky too
has its stomachs to feed and must come down
to us and learn our ways. For you do. With
splendor and work you learn how to kill and take
what you must while the salmon rot after spawning
in rain and in clarity. As we learn hovering
and density from your necessity. We learn
from you joy in the ground as you raise each
prey in your claws from the dear lost earth.

ALMA TO HER SISTER

alone no loneliness in the dream in the quiet
in the sunrise in the sunset Louise.
in the dream no loneliness in the dream
in the sunrise in the sunset just the two of us

alone no loneliness done. in the dream
in the quiet of the day done in the sunrise
Louise. in the dream in the dream
in the sunrise in the sunset.

alone no loneliness done. no loneliness
in the dream in the quiet
in the sunrise in the sunset. Louise
in the dream. in the sunrise in the sunset.

Alma

FOR MY FATHER,
HAROLD EDWARD GREGG

THE SCENT OF WHITE

The old ox and the ancient woman labor mightily
up the mountain with the strength of perishing.
The strength of each time maybe the last.
She hums and they blur into energy.
The mountain busies in the heat for their coming,
making an offering of herself. Up they walk,
up into the tall gown of the mountain that shows
her nakedness passionate. Dry scent of thyme
and sage and the smell of passing away.
The faint colors of white. Occasionally color
like fierce hunger, pomegranate or broom-yellow.
Emptiness as she waits, occasioned all summer
by nothing but goats.

AT HOME

Far is where I am near.
Far is where I live.
My house is in the far.
The night is still.
A dog barks from a farm.
A tiny dog not far below.
The bark is soft and small.
A lamp keeps the stars away.
If I go out there they are.

ME AND APHRODITE
AND THE OTHER

She doesn't move and she is stronger than I am.
She makes sounds like winter. When I plead
that I can't hear, she doesn't hear
because of the power coming out of her.
She isn't pretty. Her strength is by will.
Her mind is kept small.

Maybe those months on the mountain were too much.
Aphrodite loved me and I loved her back.
Taking her pomegranates each time I climbed
that starkness. I would search all day
in the heat and would sit finally happy
in the shade of the fig tree with what
I had found of her scant, broken treasures,
the goat bells clattering around me as I looked
down through her light to the Aegean. In a daze
of weariness, reverence and clarity.

Now this older one has come. More ancient,
tougher, less complete and as fine as can be.
She has come thinking I am strong enough,
though I sit on the curbs crying
without knowledge, without control.
Sees my mouth open and my agony.
If she can, she will destroy my life.
If she can't, I'll try again to be married.

ME AND ALMA

Time holds us together with a strong hand.
Nothing is allowed to go away on its own.
Not fish, snow nor grass.
All must issue one from the other.
This woman is my flesh, my heavy bones.
She turns as if I am the tree
and Alma its leaves.
I the green the wind of her is undoing.
Soon there will be nothing so different together
as she and I. Stone and water, dirt and fern.

ALMA THINKING ABOUT MEN

I stood watching the great hulk of desire
glide within memory. Watched it move
like the only true beauty in the world. Let it pass.
Kept to the ragged path the old men made
one by one and long ago. Desire would have led me away.
My heart beats within the galaxy of this life—
restrained, limited, in love.
Understanding how some siren longings kill.
I, keeping still in my distance, surprise them
by holding my ground, singing and shouting down praise
upon them. As if I were one of them.
I, the girl who ate dirt, who wrote of the fool
hidden in the straw crying because he wanted a monkey
and some bells to make a living.
I, who looked at the drying leaves with my heart,
have learned to come back.

DAYS

Moon is hobbled and placed in a field.
Listens to cicadas and watches the cripple
walk to the restaurants to play his bagpipe
for what little they give. The goats with her
bleat and jump happily on the rocks.
She looks at the mountains she knew
and feels like weeping, but does not.
Eats leaves from the fig tree that grows
over the wall. Her reaching up and pulling
rings the bell around her neck. Maybe,
she thinks, it's the beginning of something.

SAFE AND BEAUTIFUL

Moon, you are getting worse and worse.
Lying around in pretty satin,
your hair fixed all careful like a widow.
I capture this lizard and house it
in my hands. Feel the scratching.
We look at each other between my fingers,
he as Dante and I as the ghost,
the Lost-in-the-Night, the daughter
of faith built on common ground. While you,
old moon, play safe, safe, beautiful and safe.

THE GHOSTS POEM

I

Heavy black birds flying away hard from trees
which are the color of rust that will green.
A smaller bird says his life is easy.
"I can fly over the water and return.
I feel very little. I see to it the dead
in the boats keep their arms crossed
in the correct position. They are shaken
by wind and the drift to leeward.
And when they arrive, I am there by the lilies.
I sing my highest song. They open their eyes
and memory is removed from them.
It is the final condition."

II

I used to skate on the pond and now it is water.
With the sound of hammers and scythes, scythes
and hammers all around. So what do I know?
Laurie is dying. She told her husband she's tired
of fighting. He said he'll be glad when it's over.
They are giving her a mixture of heroin and morphine
so the mother says good-bye to her friends in euphoria.
What does she see? The Acropolis in moonlight before
it decreases? The kore which resembles most of what
we have to offer? Does death carry us to speak
with the invisible? Are we carried to an ocean
where water covers our feet and then withdraws,
leaving us shivering? What does history have to say?
"Empty rooms. The dead in layers."

III

Ghosts and the old are gathered here.
Bored of being gathered without waltzes,
one asks for music and the bird says soon.
Spider comes and goes in her tunnel.
Lady, I ask, is it true you are cruel?
You are very busy. Do you make coverings
for us to wear? "I work for Death
and the power of men. If you want me less,
you know what to do," she answers.
But I am not persuaded. The sight of them
blind and groping fills me with pain.
I must help them down the stairs and on
their way. They are the best we had,
and among them are the bronze bells
of that deliberate passion which saves
what is perfection from ruin.

IV

I go to the shore and say to Death,
here I am. What power do you have
if I care only for the living?
He shows me his skirt to be inviting.
He sings his loudest song. I sing low.
Death, I sing, you are not dear.
You are nothing but a hole in the ground.
"Watch your mouth," says the spider.
But I am too excited and tell him I have
music and memories. That men and women
embrace even in stone on the old tombs.

V

Dirt road. Then under tall pines. Then grass.
Where the land slopes, the sun shines
and many flowers came up. Some right away,
some later, some finally.
While in that place which had been a pond.
There is a creek, and a dark hill of trees
beyond, with ferns from spring until October.
Last year I spent time there every day.
I weeded out the briars and my hands bled.
During the summer there were many snakes,
or one often. This is not a story.
This is how I lived. Morning glories covered
the wall, poppies lasted late into autumn.
This winter, when the snow thawed a little,
I saw through the ice the pansies.
They still had green leaves and stems
and the flowers were the same color as before.

VI

The blackness at the window turned me back
to the fire. My heart praised its warmth
and the sound it makes of a snake hissing,
as a man breathes out when struck. The room was
darkest in the corners where the ghosts were.
What is alive is everything, they said.
Death has you standing still, little sister.
We can help very little. Bird is the least
useful. Spider is really an old woman
who hides in the ground because she is poor.
But snake knows death. He has it both ways.
Escapes from his body and lives again.
His divisions and endings return on themselves.
See how he comes into the bright summer garden
when he has a choice. Snake is wonderful.

VII

There must be more than just emotion.
Longing is enough to get me where I am,
but it cannot change me from a plant
that sings into a snake which sleeps
like a doe in the sun and then slides
into the blackness we balk from.
The resonance of romance brightens
the invisible so it can be seen.
We must ascend into light to be manifest.

VIII

If we did not hold so much, I would not write.
If it were not for memories, for the ghosts
carrying the hundred clamoring moons,
I would be safe. The forests keep
saying I should not remember, but always
there is the sound of their breathing.
If it were all right just to love and die,
I would not be in this empty place
three stories up looking out on nothing
I know. If I could bind my mouth
or teach my heart despair of living,
I would not be here learning what to say.

THE NIGHT BEFORE LEAVING

We sit at the kitchen table
waiting for some opening.
For the proper handling
of good-bye.
Going deeper and deeper
into the hours, like slow divers
sinking in their heavy gear.
We look at each other, gesturing
which way to go
through the lamplight,
garbage bags, dishes in the sink
and on the table.
We surface in a kind of dream.
The boat touches ground.
Grinds onto the rocks.
We get out,
and it floats again.

MARRIAGE AND
MIDSUMMER'S NIGHT

It has been a long time now
since I stood in our dark room looking
across the court at my husband in her apartment.
Watched them make love.
She was perhaps more beautiful
from where I stood than to him.
I can say it now: She was like a vase
lit the way milky glass is lighted.
He looked more beautiful there
than I remember him the times
he entered my bed with the light behind.
It has been ten years since I sat
at the open window, my legs over the edge
and the knife close like a discarded idea.
Looked up at the Danish night,
that pale, pale sky where the birds that fly
at dawn flew on those days all night long,
black with the light behind. They were caught
by their instincts, unable to end their flight.

WINTER BIRDS

Tell me a riddle, I said, that has no answer.
That will hold us to each other fast
and forever, like dumb things
which cannot grow, that do not change us.
That let us stay here together.
What makes a web of the winter? you said.
What are the trees of the dead?
What wind blows through all that
as the moon begins her ending, her ending?
you sang. And we danced in the cow-vacant night.
Dancing and singing until our hearts grew fat.

BALANCING EVERYTHING

When I lie in bed thinking of those years, I often
remember the ships. On the Aegean especially.
Especially at night among the islands or going
to Athens. The beauty of the moon and stillness.
How hard those journeys sometimes were.
The powerful smell of vomit and urine, sweetened
coffee and crude oil when the ship struggled
against the wind. I think of the night
we were going to die in the storm trying to reach
the passenger liner. Huge waves smashing
over our little boat. Jack screaming at the captain
because he hit me in his fear. Old Greek women
hiding their heads in my lap. Like a miracle.
I talked to them with the few words I knew.
Simple things. How it would be all right.
Telling them to look at the lights of their village
at the top of the great cliffs of Santorini,
up in the dark among the stars.

THE VISITOR

She comes in and sees winter and him
alone in the apartment.
Sits at the table thinking of when
they had lived together. Seeing
what her life was like now,
Thinks how often gentleness means suffering.
She looks out at the panel of snow.
A bird lands on a wire.
He says it is a starling.
"Fat, dark bird," she says and feels sad.
It goes away and comes back.
And goes away completely.
The man has come to see her
bringing his life. To a place
she does not yet belong.
Now her life is divided between him
and John. She looks at the snow
and thinks of her warmth and its meaning.
She puts the curtain down over the dark
before returning to the man in Amherst.

FIGURES NEAR A BRIDGE

Everything formal.
The man turns around
and makes a sound.
It is a long cry.
The woman turns around
so you can see her face.
The look on her face
is the sound he made.

PICTURES OF MARRIAGE

I

It is the way Arnolfini holds his wife's hand
that helps me. His under hers.
It's not the fancy bed nor them facing us.
I am in love with their simply being together,
even so formally. Human even so.
The dance-like way they hold still. As if she
had just lifted the skirt so their feet might
begin to step in the nice music of that time.

II

The potato-eaters move according to an absence
of music. They sit so close around the table,
it's as if the hands could be exchanged.
The man's for the woman's, the boy's for the mother's.
Any of them for the tree outside.
The gnarled one with the limbs cut back so often
it seems to have wanted to hold more than it can.
The same way, somehow, that Van Gogh does not turn
from what is turned from. Not even
from those in the dim light who fold into each other,
into what they dig up to eat. Into that music.

FORGET ALL THAT

I don't want to confuse the world
anymore with songs about love.
They sound like the giant creakings
of a wooden ship that never comes
into port these days. And even if
there was one, we would be lost
before they decided who should board.
No, the air is vast on bright days,
and the sea full of myths and miseries
loose there in the transparent dark
like some relaxed dead thing pulled
and pushed. No, let us stop telling
each other stories about love.
Of naked bodies facing each other in
the room lit only because another is.
(How quietly and slowly they approach!)
Let us leave out those visions. My job
is to keep finding quiet rooms in this city.
To know one move ahead so when the owner
arrives I have a sense of real direction
as I walk to the next one,
and the one after.

If this woman is simple
do you love her less?
Is she less important?
If she looks like sadness
but is love itself
do you want not to see her?
If you see only face and hair,
don't you imagine the hands
lifted in some larger scene?
Can't you tell she will last
until the world is done?

ALMA IN THE WOODS

I show them how the snow melts from the stone
before it goes from the ground. Show them my joy
without reason over this. I show them my passion
for the white birches on the upper ground.
That whiteness in the midst of gray maples.
Those tender trees among the winter-wise evergreens.
I tell them of being seventeen and alone,
on my hands and knees with my mouth to the stream
like a deer. Not strange, but unseen.
Waking to the woods always, and that sound.
I tell them how it can be wild high in the trees
and quiet underneath where I go to see things
which are dead and singing. Seeking with my mouth
what is lowest and most forlorn. I go to where moss
and ferns give themselves to my ignorance,
making a song of themselves for me. And I sing back,
making songs from the bones of belief.

THE THING BEING MADE

Everything is black. From a distance
a figure is coming. It could be a man
but it is a woman. She is walking
wearing a kimono. She is so white
it is as if she were left unpainted.
An absence all over her. Whole but unfinished.
She turns to her left and lifts both arms,
touching her hands to her mouth.
I can't tell if she is grieving.
On the right is the sea in the blackness.
(I can tell by the noise of its hurrying.)
There is a moon, but it does not shine.
The color of old aluminum. I have seen
bright dolphins arched for a moment each,
their bodies above their dark world.

AT THE GATE IN THE
MIDDLE OF MY LIFE

I had come prepared to answer questions,
because it said there would be questions.
I could have danced or sung. Could have loved.
But it wanted intelligence. Now it asks
what can be understood but not explained
and I have nothing with me. I take off
my shoes and say this is a plate of food.
I say the wind is going the wrong way.
Say here is my face emerging into clear light
that misses the sea we departed from to join you.
Take off my jacket and say this is a goat alone.
It embraces me, weeping human tears. Dances
sadly three times around. Then three times more.

SAYING GOOD-BYE TO THE DEAD

I walk on the dirt roads being my father.
Between tobacco fields empty in February
except for the wooden stakes and the wires.
The earth is spongy after the rains
which washed the snow away. Dogs bark
near the houses around the fields.
Mountains beyond that. I clap my hands
in the air over my head, four times.
Turn on one foot around with my arms lifted.
Stop and look at the sky fast and hard.
Then walk to the bakery and buy day-old
sweet rolls to eat in my room at the hotel.

NOT SAYING MUCH

My father is dead and there is nothing left
now except ashes and a few photographs.
The men are together in the old pictures.
Two generations of them working and boxing
and playing fiddles. They were interested
mostly in how men were men. Muscle and size.
Played their music for women and the women
did not. The music of women was long ago.
Being together made the men believe somehow.
Something the United States of America could
not give them. Not even the Mississippi.
Not running away or the Civil War or farming
the plains. Not exploring or the dream of gold.
The music and standing that way together
seems to have worked. They married women
the way they made a living. And the women
married them back, without saying much,
not loving much, not singing ever.
Those I knew in California lived and died
in beauty and not enough money. But the beauty
was like a face with the teeth touching
under closed lips and the eyes still. The men
did not talk to them much, and neither time
nor that fine place gave them a sweetness.

OEDIPUS EXCEEDING

Finally Oedipus came back. Returned
as the old to the ancient. Found a stone
and sat down. Blind and blinding.
Slowly people gathered around him,
hesitant and horrified. He began.

The earth is winnowed, he said.
Put through a sieve. It is what happens
at the borders. A grinding away.
The ocean against the curving shore.
Sky against the mountain. Less rock.
Fewer trees. A reduction of whatever
bulges. A hammering.

Almost nothing of it is useful to us.
The ocean and sky laboring to make
their place. Salt wetness and the storm.
If we go forward, we go beyond.
If we return to the gentle green center,
we come back defeated. We are expected
to rejoice and grieve at the same moment.

A telling goes on at the border.
At the border an intermingling of fish
with swallow. Of eagle with hands.
I have returned to mix my blood with our
earth. Mix myself with what we are not.
(His voice in the crowd was like wind

blowing the chaff away.) There is a hole
in the ground behind this stone, he said,
through the bushes. I will go there now
and lie down forever.

The people walked back toward town.
Something had happened. Everything
was sacred. Air, goat, plants, people.
All full of worship. Bodies, torsos, legs,
minds full of worship. And strong enough
to be happy in the elements.

THE SHOPPING-BAG LADY

You told people I would know easily what the murdered
lady had in her sack which could prove she was happy
more or less. As if they were a game, the old women
who carry all they own in bags, maybe proudly,
without homes we think except the streets.
But if I could guess (nothing in sets for example),
I would not. They are like those men who lay their
few things on the ground in a park at the end of Hester.
For sale perhaps, but who can tell? Like her way
of getting money. Never asking. Sideways and disconcerting.
With no thanks, only judgment. "You are a nice girl,"
one said as she moved away and then stopped in front
of a bum sitting on the bench who yelled that he would
kill her if she did not get away from him. She walked
at an angle not exactly away but until she was the same
distance from each of us. Stood still, looking down.
Standing in our attention as if it were a palpable thing.
Like the city itself or the cold winter. Holding her hands.
And if there was disgrace, it was God's. The failure
was ours as she remained quiet near the concrete wall
with cars coming and the sound of the subway filling
and fading in the most important place we have yet devised.

LIES AND LONGING

Half the women are asleep on the floor
on pieces of cardboard.
One is facedown under a blanket
with her feet and ankle bracelet showing.
Her spear leans against the wall by her head
where she can reach it.
The woman who sits on a chair won't speak
because this is not her dress.
An old woman sings an Italian song in English
and says she wants her name in lights:
Faye Runaway. Tells about her grown children.
One asks for any kind of medicine.
One says she has a rock that means honor
and a piece of fur.
One woman's feet are wrapped in rags.
One keeps talking about how fat she is
so nobody will know she's pregnant.
They lie about getting letters.
One lies about a beautiful dead man.
One lies about Denver. Outside
it's Thirtieth Street and hot and no sun.

HOW THE JOY OF IT
WAS USED UP LONG AGO

No one standing.
No one for a long time.
The room is his room,
but he does not go there.
Because of the people.
He stands in the dark hall.
The smell makes him close
his eyes, but not move
from the place so near.
They have cut the cow open
and climb into the ooze
and pulse of its great body.
The man is noble, the festival
growing louder in his flesh.
His face is sad with thinking
of how to think about it,
while his mind is slipping
into the fat woman.
The one he saw for a moment
near day, open and asleep.
A filth on the floor of that room.

WHAT THEY ATE WHAT
THEY WORE

We see the dog running
and it excites us dimly
as if our lives were important.
The living dog and not
the idea of having one.
Like when my mind sees them
building that great wall
through China and I wonder
where they slept. Huts
with reed roofs or caves in stone.
And what they thought it meant.
I was telling an old farmer
who gave me a ride last month
I might have a job picking apples.
Be sure to wear gloves, he said.
The apples are very cold in the morning.

COMING HOME

I see no way to survive the soul's journey.
At the beginning, we are like angels
painted around the Madonna. Conceived
in safety, in the freshness of our bodies.
As we age, wisdom can be heard climbing
the stairs blindly under the bare bulb
groping for a string which we know how
to find in the dark only if we have
practiced delicately meanwhile.

THE MEN LIKE SALMON

The heart does not want to go up.
The bones whip it there, driving it
with a terrible music of the spirit.
The flesh falls off like language,
bruised and sick. Sick with the bones.
Rotten with sorrow. Leaving everything
good or loved behind. The bones
want to go. To end like Christ.
Ah, the poor flesh. The mute sound
of flesh against stone. Emptied
of maidens and summer and all
the fine wantonness of life.
The bones insist on immaculate changes.
The women stand to the side remembering
Io with vicious flies close to her heart.

LOVERS

He keeps her away, thinking they know each other
too much. Thinking it will be good again with her
if he stays away long enough again.
As in the old days when they knew nothing
of each other and were intimate,
as one enters a field of wind alone.
She makes songs and things and is pleased
but understands that angels sad and poor fill
the place of absence, of people, and of lovers
if there were any. Lovers, as the wind calls
desire and means those who never know each other.

THE COPPERHEAD

Almost blind he takes the soft dying
into the muscle-hole of his haunting.
The huge jaws eyeing, the raised head sliding
back and forth, judging the exact place of his killing.
He does not know his burden. He is not so smart.
He does not know his feelings. He only knows
his sliding and the changing of his hunger.
He waits. He sleeps. He looks but does not know his
seeing. He only knows the smallness of a moving.
He does not see the fear of the trapping.
He only sees the moving. He does not feel the caution.
He does not question. He only feels the flexing
and rearing of his wanting. He goes forward
where he is eyeing and knows the fastness
of his mouthing. He does not see the quickness collapsing.
He does not see at all what he has done. He only feels
the newness of his insides. The soft thing moving.
He does not see the moving. He is busy coaxing
and dreaming and feeling the softness moving in him.
The inside of him feels like another world.
He takes the soft thing and coaxes it
away from his small knowing. He would turn in and follow,
hunt it deep within the dark hall of his fading knowing,
but he cannot. He knows that.
That he cannot go deep within his body for the finding
of the knowing. So he slows and lets go. And finds
with his eyes a moving. A small moving that he knows.

DEATH LOOKS DOWN

Death looks down on the salmon.
A male and female in two pools, one above
the other. The female turns back along the path
of water to the male, does not touch him,
and returns to the place she had been.

I know what death will do. Their bodies already
are sour and ragged. Blood has risen
to the surface under the scales. One side
of his jaw is unhinged. Death will pick them up.
Put them under his coat against his skin
and belt them there. Will walk away
up the path through the bay trees.
Through the dry grass of California to where
the mountain begins. Where a few deer
almost the color of the hills will look up
until he is under the trees again and the road ends
and there is a gate. He will climb over that
with his treasure. It
will be dark by then.

But for now he does nothing. He does not disturb
the silence at all. Nor the occasional sound
of leaves, of ferns touching, of grass or stream.
For now he looks down at the salmon large and whole
motionless days and nights in the cold water.
Lying still, always facing the constant motion.

PRESSURE AGAINST EMPTINESS

Apollo's left fist covers his heart.
His eyes are holes. He used to shine,
but time has darkened him.
His bronze thighs are covered with words.
He is waist-deep in language.
I see wheat, lust-teacher, tree-darkness.
Goat, mountain, river, tree-in-a-field.
Was he merged with life?
Was he ripeness holding still?
Did he say, this is my body, eat me?
Was he strength made out of pity?
He has the pierced, blank look of love,
knowing we die as flowers do
and it makes a difference, a pressure
against emptiness. Did they know him?
Did the shining change their bones?
At night they knew the grass by touch.
When day began to end they heard owls.
Away in the fields and within their bodies.

CHOOSING AGAINST RUINS

I thought the old statue was a kore,
but it's probably Artemis.
Either of them is almost gone.
Love has worn her down to mere stone,
past her time of clarity.
Rough to the breasts and then smooth
down to the feet.
She has stopped being a woman,
is a generality of form.
Which does not delight me nowadays.
I have returned to the ocean
too many times to care what survives
the rising or fails the thrust.
It was flourishing she stayed for:
made briefly moon-bright under
the sycamore tree by the brook
to give strength to the world.
That time came and passed.
She grew into a woman.
Stood quiet and straight.
Then rain fell. The rain fell and fell.
Now there is only a possibility
she remains. A shadow of stone.

INNOCENTS

The dahlias are tied up straight
in the German garden in Russia
and the mistress is walking there
with small steps. Ah, someone is
always managing. Not the very rich,
but one of the servants.
Poor Akim has lost everything
and now is called drunk because
of his grief by the pious man
who has given him a lift in the cart.
After two days the cart comes on
Akim's wife who throws herself crying
on the ground saying he should kill her.
Saying the man she ran off with
took her and then threw her away.
That was the man who ruined Akim.
She thought it was love. Yesterday
the moon came up red, making a dark shade
for the lovers. The man came out of it
rich all in one day. Maybe the moon
is like the servant in a stiff white hat
who manages the rich lady. Who in turn
manages the son who orders cruelty
for those who have suffered the most
and have nothing.

WHAT IS LEFT OVER

There is silence after a city is destroyed
the Russian woman told me. For those left,
there are potatoes which might grow soon
enough. No pigeons and no rats. All eaten.
The brother who died was eating cooked water
from a spoon that distant morning.
Josef, hearing it again, cut his hand
and the party ended. The vodka was drunk
and the two kinds of caviar eaten.
I never understood what they were celebrating
in the first place. He told me to go up
and get into his bed. He was talking Russian
angrily at her as I went up the stairs.
She had said the city was like a stage set
for the few people. That her mother built
a shed against the palace portico,
keeping her eyes on the garden so no one
could steal the potato plants.

SOMETHING SCARY

Over the phone Joel tells me
his marriage is suddenly miraculous.
That his wife is glad now about us.
Is even grateful.
"We have crossed a border," he says.
I listen, knowing myself too far gone
to last more than a day.
Remembering him in that dark room
with the shades down saying,
"You don't need the sun. You carry
a brightness in you." And me saying
nothing, burning alone lying there
like the terrible brightness of heaven.

NEW YORK ADDRESS

The sun had just gone out
and I was walking three miles to get home.
I wanted to die.
I couldn't think of words and I had no future
and I was coming down hard on everything.
My walk was terrible.
I didn't seem to have a heart at all
and my whole past seemed filled up.
So I started answering all the questions
regardless of consequence:
Yes I hate dark. No I love light. Yes I won't speak.
No I will write. Yes I will breed. No I won't love.
Yes I will bless. No I won't close. Yes I won't give.
Love is on the other side of the lake.
It is painful because the dark makes you hear
the water more. I accept all that.
And that we are not allowed romance but only its distance.
Having finished with it all, now I am not listening.
I wait for the silence to resume.

I WILL REMEMBER

I will remember making love last night.
I thought when you rolled on your back
we would not. You halted my hand
on your arm, just touching my fingers.
But then something happened and we were
all of a sudden part of the same weight.

ALMA IN THE DARK

She reaches over and puts a hand on his hipbone
and presses. He turns softly away and she makes
his shape against the back. Her arm around
the waist covering his unguarded stomach.
He does not wake. Her heart in its nest
sings foolishly. It is awake and happy
and useless at this time. Saying dumb things
like *The stone house is firm*
or *The almond tree is blown around in the wind.*

CHILDREN AMONG THE HILLS

The lamb was so skinny I thought it was a baby goat
and called my sister to see. Lying on his side,
legs straight out in front, little stomach pulsing.
The head lifted, sideways, and began telling us
how much he hated the promiscuous sun which shines
on all things equally. Rotting one, growing strength
in another. On those caged in virtue and on men who
walk through the streets at ease in the hot light.
On that which is not quite animal, on what is not
quite mineral. That which hisses in the shadows
along the wall. Army of horses practicing formations
in the Swiss mountains. Shepherds fleeing into Italy.
On the two dead fish on the sidewalk still pink from
their life in the sea. Finally the lamb slept.
The trees on the hills around us were silent.
Inside everything was moving, shivering with wind.

DRY GRASS & OLD COLOR OF THE
FENCE & SMOOTH HILLS

The women are at home in this California town.
The eucalyptus trees move against whiteness.
When a mother comes by I touch the child's face
over and over, sliding my hand lightly down,
and each time he smiles. All life is beautiful
at a distance. But when I sit in their houses,
it's all mess and canning and babies crying.
I hear over and over the stories about their men:
betrayal, indifference, power. Age without passion,
boys without fathers. My sister lives between.
She cleans her house. She names all the roses
she shows me. She turns on the record and we dance.
She inside with the door open, me on the porch.
Later her boyfriend arrives. The one who hits her,
and steals her money, and gets drunk. Etcetera.
They have sex. In the morning we're alone and she
wants to know if I want waffles with raspberry jam.

TRYING TO BELIEVE

There's nothing gentle where Aphrodite was.
Empty mountain and grasshoppers banging
into me. Maybe there never was.
But I go up again and again to search
under thornbushes and rocks.
Am grateful for the marble arm
big as my thumb. A shard with a man's feet
and a shard with the feet of a bird. A sign
that it can be more. Like when a wind comes
in the great heat and lifts at my body.
Like when I get back to my mountain, aching
and my hands hurt. Sit alone looking down at
evening on the ocean, drinking wine or not.

IF DEATH WANTS ME

If death wants me, let it come.
I am here in a room at night on my own.
The pulsing and the crickets would go on.
Everything and the tall trees bathed in darkness
would continue. I am here with the lights on
writing my last words. If he does not come,
I will still be here doing the same thing.
Things change outside of me. Rain is falling
fast in the quiet. My love got on a boat
and it went away. I stayed. When the moon rose,
I tilted my head to the side when she did.
When people came, I felt a little crazy.
I did what I remembered. Made food.
Asked questions and responded. And they left.
I would go to sleep and wake in the sun.
Love the day as if it were a host of memories,
then go to the wall and wait.
That hour was perhaps the finest of all.
No people. No bright face. No geese walking home.
No night sounds at all. I was silent
with all things around coming and leaving
in abeyance on their journeying. I would sing
a song for them all. This is for you
and this is for you. And then the moon would slide up
over the hill and I would be captured in her light
like a growing thing, gone and complete.

THE RIVER AGAIN AND AGAIN

If we stayed together long enough to see
the seasons return, to see the young animals
and the opening of peonies and summer heat,
then we could make sense of the hawk's calm
or the deer. I could show you how repetition
helps us to understand the truth.
And we would know one another sometimes
with a love that touches indifference.

WITH A BLESSING RATHER
THAN LOVE SAID NIETZSCHE

The square stone room makes a shape in the air
to rest inside. A form for holding what is loved
beyond naming. With gratitude and reverence
as Nietzsche. We have other ways,
other places. Like figs left on the stone shelf
above the patio as a gift.
You go out and return with fruit you've picked
and I make jam for our crepes and yogurt
and we eat. It is still morning and we look
at each other even though we have known each other
for years. You take me on your lap
in the chair by the open window and pull off
the shirts over our heads so we can feel the air
and embrace and kiss high up on the mountain,
in the shaded room by the screen window
where the air keeps touching us
and we are happy beyond saying, beyond
any sounds even. Less than nothing and deeper.

LESSENING

Without even looking in the album
I realized suddenly, two months later,
you had stolen the picture of me.
The one in color in the Greek waves.
After you had hurt me so much,
how could you also take the picture
from me of a time before I knew you?
When I was with Jack.
Steal the small proof that once
I lived well, was loved
and beautiful.

WHITE LIGHT

Waiting in a place where the cicadas turn the silence
into something silver. Hot light on the rocks.
Laurel down by the spring. Holding myself still.
Doing one thing at a time. Drink water, burn paper,
wash floor. The sun makes me lower my eyes to see
when I am outdoors. Wind turns the leaves
hour after hour. View of water far below.
Town far below by the water.
Sky beyond the next island.
Loneliness goes out as far as I can see.

ADULT

I've come back to the country where I was happy
changed. Passion puts no terrible strain on me now.
I wonder what will take the place of desire.
I could be the ghost of my own life returning
to the places I lived best. Walking here and there,
nodding when I see something I cared for deeply.
Now I'm in my house listening to the owls calling
and wondering if slowly I will take on flesh again.

STILL, ATTENTIVE, CLENCHED

The fir, poplar and eucalyptus around the house
move each in its own way in the same wind.
Then a man comes easily through the trees
with some urgent duty, like Hermes with his orders
memorized. He is fearsome because he does not care
about me personally. Merely wants.
He calls and I do not answer. It is like war.
He knocks on the door and I slide down the wall.
Hug my knees, hear my breathing. He walks around
to the windows and I lie on my stomach.
He calls my name. He does not tell me why he has come.
The lights are out, but he can see the fire is burning.
I know he knows I am there. Knows how much I am afraid.

NOT WANTING HERSELF

Not wanting herself, she tries to go
into whatever makes longing:
the hawks mating and falling,
the Sung paintings where the Chinese
live in their own distance.
Wrenching to get away,
she puts down money
to go into the dark place
and see advertisements of her desires.
But they hit her. Hit her
when she wanted to see the birds fly.
Birds who are part of herself
with hearts you can eat.
They invade her longing
with an intelligence that does not hold
on to anything. Ah, dreams,
she is losing even you.
The only lover her mind has left
separates her mind like milk.

SASKIA AND ALMA GO
DIFFERENT WAYS

My life was already desperate when she got sick.
When Saskia lay down that night, she was wet
under the chin and she might die. She was weak
and her teeth showed. She didn't push against me
with her feet. She didn't eat my hair.

My feet were bare when I saw her dead.
My blanket was still warm when I took her down
the wooden steps to the grass and the fig tree
and buried her in the ground. I was on my hands
and knees putting what I love over the body.
A leaf fell on her from the tree.

I hold on to so many things. When I lived on the island,
I climbed the vacant mountain again and again
to put fruit on the rocks where Aphrodite had been.
My friend Michiko sat gentle at her table
under the cypress on the other mountain and did not live
long after she left. I hold my mother, the earth and cows.
We go by ship, bicycle, by owl to get beyond ourselves,
beyond this world. To include the other, and fail.

Or get only a little. I carry ashes across this snow
and dump them on the place that will sink down
when the whiteness is gone. Some of the ashes blow
a small distance, making a stain. I remember

the woman in Kurosawa's film after they lost the battle
with something on her back looking for people
she knew by their absence, as the planet was found
because of the force of the invisible.

I sat in Portsmouth Square after Saskia, my rabbit, died,
watching the Chinese man talk crazy to me as long
as I faced him. Between him and the row of pines
(with poplars behind), a man sat on the concrete shaking
as Saskia did, marring the lotus he was making. The trees
are good, I thought, even though they don't shine.

I went at random into a store directly behind me.
A man came forward and asked, What do you want?
What do you have? I said. I sell things
for the living and the dead, he answered. And I said,
I want to buy those things. Two women at the rear
were eating soup, sucking on the crab shells. I bought
a pink dress made of paper with pomegranates on it.
Paper things of red with green and black and yellow.
I bought money for the ghosts and spirits,
remembering the fig leaf falling that morning
just before I covered her with dirt. A day I touched
life twice. One real, one of paper. One for myself,
one for both realms which want to touch.

That was the religious part. But Saskia is dead
and might die. By fear and memory. She might die
and that softness go away. Nothing to be done.
The fog comes in. Can we let memory suffice? Is it
possible to keep the body with itself? Hands holding dirt.
The poplar trees not shining behind the dark pines.
The man on the concrete shivering. The custard pie I ate
after, which cost sixty cents in the Chinese coffee shop.

Custard and coffee and memory and presence. The spirit
of her soft fur and the body hardened by death.
Myself who isn't anything stopped yet. Who must learn
everything over because she is another with my memory.
Taken away. Mostly lost. The geraniums I put on her,
paper heart, paper fish, lots of mint. Five-fingered fern
and the leaf that fell from the tree by itself.
My heart is vacant. My position like a rabbit.
My eyes vacant, blurring her in the light.

ALMA IS WILLING

She is willing to grow larger. Put forth leaves
and apples. Preside over disputes of snake with man.
Symbolize with her life the ruin of time's management.
She is half the material of happiness.
Half a symbol of the best things destroyed. All of this
because her roots are underneath the earth
while her eminence is high and the sun holds her to it.
To its ride and rule. So she must choose and choose,
die and regain the muscle and purity of everything.
Harvest apples in the fall before frost comes
to turn the firm fruit to mush.
Fragility even in something so good and round.

PRAISING SPRING

The day is taken by each thing and grows complete.
I go out and come in and go out again,
confused by a beauty that knows nothing of delay,
rushing like fire. All things move faster
than time and make a stillness thereby. My mind
leans back and smiles, having nothing to say.
Even at night I go out with a light and look
at the growing. I kneel and look at one thing
at a time. A white spider on a peony bud.
I have nothing to give, and make a poor servant,
but I can praise the spring. Praise this wildness
that does not heed the hour. The doe that does not
stop at dark but continues to grow all night long.
The beauty in every degree of flourishing. Violets
lift to the rain and the brook gets louder than ever.
The old German farmer is asleep and the flowers go on
opening. There are stars. Mint grows high. Leaves
bend in the sunlight as the rain continues to fall.

TWELVE YEARS AFTER THE MARRIAGE SHE TRIES TO EXPLAIN HOW SHE LOVES HIM NOW

Beyond the mountain is a meadow with iris.
The shade of the firs determines the measure
of their color. Violet so pure the purple
is almost not there. The difference
between air and the sky's blue.
The iris hold color because they are a thing,
but mysteriously, making both the substance
and the invisible more clear.

THE WOMAN ON HER KNEES
AT THE RIVER

She is washing clothes,
her body moving forward
and back in its two positions.
Suppliant giving. She grinds corn
with stone on stone the same way
and makes the round flat bread.
All this in a place filled with
the weight of death.
Life would stop in this poverty
if she got into a boat that moved
away by itself full of flowers.

LINDA GREGG is the author of seven books of poetry, including *All of It Singing: New and Selected Poems,* which received the Jackson Poetry Prize from Poets & Writers, the Lenore Marshall Poetry Prize from the Academy of American Poets, the William Carlos Williams Award from the Poetry Society of America, and the American Book Award from the Before Columbus Foundation. Gregg has received fellowships from the Guggenheim Foundation, the Lannan Foundation, and the National Endowment for the Arts. She received the PEN/Voelcker Award in Poetry for achievement across her career. She lives in New York City.

The text of this book is set in Adobe Garamond,
drawn by Robert Slimbach and based on type cut by
Claude Garamond in the sixteenth century.
Book design by Wendy Holdman.
Typesetting by Stanton Publication Services, Inc.
Manufactured by BookMobile on
acid-free 30 percent postconsumer wastepaper.